Bird Babies

Catherine Veitch

Heinemann
LIBRARY
Chicago, Illinois

Edited by Daniel Nunn, Rebecca Rissman,
and Catherine Veitch
Designed by Cynthia Della-Rovere
Picture research by Ruth Blair
Production by Victoria Fitzgerald
Originated by Capstone Global Library

Library of Congress Cataloging-in-Publication Data

Veitch, Catherine.
 Bird babies / Catherine Veitch.
    pages cm.—(Animal babies)
 Includes bibliographical references and index.
 ISBN 978-1-4329-7492-3 (hb)
 ISBN 978-1-4329-8417-5 (pb)
 1.Birds—Infancy—Juvenile literature. I. Title.
 QL676.2.V45 20134
 598.13'92—dc23   2012033022

Acknowledgments
Alamy: Cultura RM, 17; Nature Picture Library:
BERNARD CASTELEIN, 21, Grzegorz Lesniewski, 9,
23 (middle), John Downer, 19, MIKE READ, 14, Paul
Johnson, 13, Stephen Dalton, 15, Yuri Shibnev, 7, 23
(top); Shutterstock: Bambuh, 10, Cheryl E. Davis, 22
(right), Craig Barhorst, 22 (top), Frank Pali, 12, J.A.Astor,
11, Janneke Spronk, 20, Jaroslaw Saternus, 5, Josh
Anon, 18, Maksimilian, 6, rawcaptured, 23 (bottom),
Stephanie Dalen, 4, Steve Byland, back cover, 16,
thomas bonnefoy1, 22 (left), Vishnevskiy Vasily, 2, 8, 22
(bottom); SuperStock: Martin Rgner/Westend6, cover, 1

We would like to thank Michael Bright for his invaluable
help in the preparation of this book.

Every effort has been made to contact copyright holders
of any material reproduced in this book. Any omissions
will be rectified in subsequent printings if notice is given
to the publisher.

Contents

What Is a Bird?

beak

feathers

A bird has a beak.

A bird has feathers.

wings

A bird has wings.
Most birds can fly.

How Are Baby Birds Born?

egg

Female birds lay eggs.

Some birds lay one egg at a time.

Some birds lay more than one egg at a time.

Eggs can be different colors.
Eggs can be different sizes.

A baby bird hatches from each egg.

feathers

Some baby birds are born
with feathers.

Some baby birds are born with
no feathers.

Where Do Baby Birds Live?

Most baby birds live in nests.

Nests help keep them safe.

Some baby birds live in nests on the ground.

Some baby birds live in nests
on cliffs.

Some baby birds live in nests
in buildings.

What Do Baby Birds Eat?

Some baby birds are fed by their parents.

Many baby birds eat worms. Many baby birds eat seeds and berries.

Caring for Eggs and Baby Birds

A bird protects its eggs and baby birds from predators.

oil

This bird spits a smelly oil at predators to scare them away.

Growing Up

Baby birds learn to fly.

Sometimes they fall out of the nest.

Baby birds learn to find food.

Life Cycle of a Bird

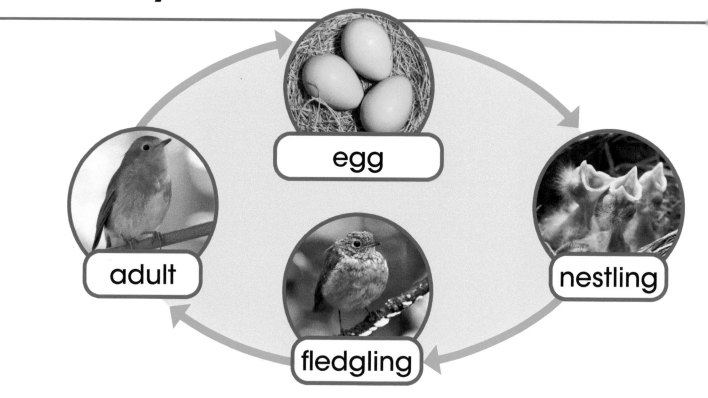

egg

nestling

fledgling

adult

A life cycle shows the different stages of an animal's life. This is the life cycle of a bird.

Picture Glossary

female animal that can give birth. Female birds lay eggs.

hatch break out of an egg

predator animal that eats other animals

Index

Notes to Parents and Teachers

Before reading

Show children a collection of photos and videos of birds. National Geographic and PBS are useful websites. Explain what a bird is and discuss the characteristics of birds.

After reading

- Mount photos of adult and baby birds on note cards and play games of concentration where the children have to match a baby bird with its parent. Model the correct pairs first.
- Ask children to label the parts of a bird: for example, beak, feathers, wings, legs.
- Look at page 22 and discuss the life cycle stages of a bird. Mount photos of the egg, nestling, fledgling, and adult stages and ask children to put the photos in order. Encourage children to draw a life cycle of a human to compare. Compare how different birds care for their babies. Discuss the care human babies need.
- To extend children's knowledge, the birds are as follows: peacock: p. 4; barn owl: p. 5; puffin: p. 6; finch eggs: p. 7; gull hatching: p. 9; emu: p. 10; chickadee: p. 11; hummingbird: p. 12; oystercatcher: p. 13; kittiwake: p. 14; swallows: p. 15; eastern bluebirds: p. 16; robin: p. 17; cormorants: p. 18; fulmar: p. 19; wagtail: p. 20; avocet: p. 21.